W0099559

Cambridge Young Learners English Tests

Cambridge Flyers 7

Answer Booklet

Examination papers from

University of Cambridge
ESOL Examinations:

English for Speakers of Other Languages

CAMBRIDGE
UNIVERSITY PRESS

CAMBRIDGE UNIVERSITY PRESS
Cambridge, New York, Melbourne, Madrid, Cape Town,
Singapore, São Paulo, Delhi, Mexico City

Cambridge University Press
The Edinburgh Building, Cambridge CB2 8RU, UK

www.cambridge.org
Information on this title: www.cambridge.org/9780521173766

© Cambridge University Press 2011

This publication is in copyright. Subject to statutory exception
and to the provisions of relevant collective licensing agreements,
no reproduction of any part may take place without the written
permission of Cambridge University Press.

First published 2011
Reprinted 2012

Printed in Poland by Opolgraf

A catalogue record for this publication is available from the British Library

ISBN 978-0-521-17375-9 Student's Book
ISBN 978-0-521-17376-6 Answer Booklet
ISBN 978-0-521-17377-3 Audio CD

Cover design by David Lawton
Produced by Peter & Jan Simmonett

Cambridge University Press has no responsibility for the persistence or
accuracy of URLs for external or third-party internet websites referred to in
this publication, and does not guarantee that any content on such websites is,
or will remain, accurate or appropriate. Information regarding prices, travel
timetables and other factual information given in this work is correct at
the time of first printing but Cambridge University Press does not guarantee
the accuracy of such information thereafter.

Contents

Introduction

The *Cambridge Young Learners English Tests* offer an elementary-level testing system (up to CEFR level A2) for learners of English between the ages of 7 and 12. The tests include 3 key levels of assessment: *Starters*, *Movers* and *Flyers*.

Flyers is the third level in the system. Test instructions are very simple and consist only of words and structures specified in the syllabus.

The complete test lasts about one hour and a quarter and has the following components: Listening, Reading and Writing, and Speaking.

	length	number of parts	number of questions
Listening	approx. 25 minutes	5	25
Reading and Writing	40 minutes	7	50
Speaking	approx. 7–9 minutes	4	–

Candidates need a pen or pencil for the Reading and Writing paper, and coloured pens or pencils for the Listening paper. All answers are written on the question papers.

Listening

In general, the aim is to focus on the 'here and now' and to use language in meaningful contexts. In addition to multiple-choice and short-answer questions, candidates are asked to use coloured pencils to mark their responses to one task. There are 5 parts. Each part begins with a clear example.

part	main skill focus	input	expected response	number of questions
1	the main skill focus in all five parts of the Listening test is listening for specific information of various kinds, e.g. numbers, describing people etc.	picture, names and dialogue	draw lines to match names to people in a picture	5
2		form or page of notepad with missing words and dialogue	write words or numbers in gaps	5
3		picture sets and list of illustrated words or names and dialogue	match pictures with illustrated word or name by writing letter in box	5
4		3-option multiple-choice pictures and dialogues	tick box under correct picture	5
5		picture and dialogue	carry out instructions to colour, draw and write (range of colours is: black, blue, brown, green, grey, orange, pink, purple, red, yellow)	5

Reading and Writing

Again, the focus is on the 'here and now' and the use of language in meaningful contexts where possible. To complete the test, candidates need a single pen or pencil of any colour. There are 7 parts, each starting with a clear example.

part	main skill focus	input	expected response	number of questions
1	reading definitions and matching to words copying words	nouns and definitions	copy the correct words next to the definitions	10
2	reading sentences about a picture and writing one-word answers	picture and sentences	write 'yes' or 'no'	7
3	reading and completing a continuous dialogue	half a dialogue with responses in a box	select correct response and write A–H in gap	5
4	reading for specific information and gist copying words	gapped text with words in a box	choose and copy missing words correctly tick a box to choose the best title for the story	6
5	reading and understanding a story completing sentences	story, picture and gapped sentences	complete sentences about story by writing 1, 2, 3 or 4 words	7
6	reading story copying words	gapped text and 3-option multiple choice (grammatical words)	complete text by selecting the correct words and copying them in corresponding gaps	10
7	reading and understanding a short text (e.g. page from diary or letter) providing words	gapped text	write words in gaps no answer options given	5

Speaking

In the Speaking test, the candidate speaks with 1 examiner for about 8 minutes. The format of the test is explained in advance to the child in their native language, by a teacher or person familiar to them. This person then takes the child into the exam room and introduces them to the examiner.

Speaking ability is assessed according to various criteria, including comprehension, the ability to produce a prompt, appropriate and accurate response, and pronunciation.

part	main skill focus	input	expected response
1	understanding statements and responding with differences	two (one is the examiner's) similar pictures oral statements about examiner's picture	identify six differences in candidate's picture from oral statements about Examiner's picture
2	responding to questions with short answers and forming questions to elicit information	one set of facts and one set of question cues	answer and ask questions about two people, objects or situations
3	understanding the beginning of a story and then continuing it based on a series of pictures	picture sequence	describe each picture in turn
4	understanding and responding to personal questions	open-ended questions about candidate	answer personal questions

Further information

The topics, structures, words and tasks upon which the *Cambridge Young Learners English Tests* are based are comprehensively described in the Handbook, so teachers or parents can know exactly what to expect.

Further information about the *Cambridge Young Learners English Tests* can be obtained from the Centre Exams Manager for Cambridge ESOL examinations in your area, or from:

University of Cambridge ESOL Examinations
1 Hills Road
Cambridge CB1 2EU
United Kingdom

Telephone: +44 1223 553997
Fax: +44 1223 553621

e-mail: ESOLHelpdesk@CambridgeESOL.org
www.CambridgeESOL.org

Test 1 Answers

Listening

Part 1 (5 marks)
Lines should be drawn between:
1 Emma and the girl who has dropped a plate
2 Betty and the baby girl crying on the floor
3 Richard and the man leaving the room, holding a newspaper
4 Helen and the girl sitting on the sofa, eating sweets
5 David and the boy sitting at the table, listening to CDs

Part 2 (5 marks)
1 History/history   2 dentist   3 meeting (at South Television)
4 Follow   5 Saffron (correct spelling)

Part 3 (5 marks)
1 Alex – B – airport   2 Fred – A – chemist's shop
3 Lucy – E – theatre   4 Katy – D – home
5 Paul – H – factory

Part 4 (5 marks)
1 B   2 B   3 A   4 C   5 A

Part 5 (5 marks)
1 Colour the bigger snowman at the front – yellow
2 Colour the trousers of the child next to the skis, throwing snowballs – brown
3 Write 'ICE' under 'THIN' on the board
4 Draw a house on top of the smaller mountain (further away), and colour it – purple
5 Colour the jacket of the girl riding her bike over the bridge – green

TRANSCRIPT   *Hello. This is the Cambridge Flyers Practice Listening Test, Test 1.*

Part 1   *Listen and look. There is one example.*

[pause]

WOMAN: Your house is very noisy!
BOY: Yes, it's always like this.
WOMAN: Who are all the people? What are their names?
BOY: Well, the little boy who's playing the drum is my brother. He's called Sam.

[pause]

Can you see the line? This is an example. Now you listen and draw lines.

[pause]

1

WOMAN: Look, that girl has dropped a plate.
BOY: Oh dear. Poor Emma! She made that pizza for her lunch.
WOMAN: Why doesn't someone help her?
BOY: Mm. Everyone's busy.

[pause]

2

WOMAN: Who's the child on the floor?
BOY: The boy who's watching television?
WOMAN: No, not him. The baby girl. She's crying loudly.
BOY: Oh, yes. That's my little cousin, Betty.
WOMAN: She wants to play the drum too, I think.

[pause]

3

WOMAN: That man looks angry.

BOY: Who? The one who's going out of the room?

WOMAN: Yes.

BOY: That's Richard. He's my uncle. It's too noisy for him.

WOMAN: Mm. He can't read his newspaper.

[pause]

4

BOY: Can you see the girl who's watching television?

WOMAN: The one behind the sofa?

BOY: No, the one who's sitting on the sofa and eating sweets.

WOMAN: OK, yes.

BOY: Her name's Helen. She's my older sister.

WOMAN: She's enjoying the programme, isn't she?

BOY: Yes, it's her favourite.

[pause]

5

WOMAN: Who's that boy who's sitting at the table?

BOY: That's my friend, David. It was his birthday last week, and I gave him a new CD.

WOMAN: The music's loud, isn't it?

BOY: Yes. And he plays it again and again and again!

[pause]

Now listen to Part 1 again.

[The recording is repeated.]

[pause]

That is the end of Part 1.

[pause]

Part 2   *Listen and look. There is one example.*

[pause]

GIRL: Mum. Can my friend Daisy come here after school on Monday?

WOMAN: Not on Monday, Jane. You're going to Vicky's house, remember?

GIRL: Oh, yes, of course. I forgot. I'm going to look after her baby.

WOMAN: Look, I'm writing it in the family diary, so you won't forget.

[pause]

Can you see the answer? Now you listen and write.

[pause]

GIRL: Oh, can you write something for me, under Tuesday?

WOMAN: Yes. What shall I write?

GIRL: 'Jane's History Exam.'

WOMAN: Ooh, yes. That's important.

GIRL: And something else. Jack has to go to the doctor's on Wednesday morning. He told me.

WOMAN: Your brother Jack gets everything wrong! He has to go to the dentist then. I've told him three times.

GIRL: When is Dad going to go to London?

WOMAN: On Thursday morning, very early. He's going to fly this time.

GIRL: Really? What's he going to do there?

WOMAN: He has an important meeting at South Television.

GIRL: Oh, right. Mum, could we go to the cinema on Friday evening?

WOMAN: Um, yes, all right. There's a new film with Sally Gold – what's it called – 'Find That Star'?

GIRL: No, Mum. It's 'Follow That Star'.

WOMAN: Well, let's go and see that.

GIRL: Could we go to a restaurant before the film starts?

WOMAN: No, Jane. We're going out for dinner on Saturday, remember? For your father's birthday.

GIRL: Oh, yes. Sorry. Where are we going to go?

WOMAN: To the Saffron Restaurant. Ooh, how do you spell that?

GIRL: Oh, Mum – it's S-A-double F-R-O-N. And they have really good mango ice cream there.

WOMAN: I know. It's your father's favourite, too!

[pause]

Now listen to Part 2 again.

[The recording is repeated.]

[pause]

That is the end of Part 2.

[pause]

Part 3   *Listen and look. There is one example.*

[pause]

Where do John's old school friends work?

[pause]

MAN: Here are my old school photos. Look – this was my class, 25 years ago! I still see some of these people.

GIRL: What do they do now?

MAN: Well, this boy here (he's a man now, of course!) is called Michael. I see him every day because he works with me at the bank.

[pause]

Can you see the letter G? Now you listen and write a letter in each box.

[pause]

GIRL: What about this girl here?

MAN: Alex? Mm. She was very clever and she studied Science. Now she has a very good job at the city airport. I still see her sometimes because we play tennis together.

[pause]

GIRL: Who's the boy with the red hair?

MAN: His name's Fred. He was very funny. At school he often said to us, "One day, I'm going to be a clown and work in a circus." Well, I met him again two months ago, and he does something very different from that. He sells medicines to people, in a chemist's shop. He hasn't got much red hair now, but he still makes me laugh!

[pause]

GIRL: What's this girl's name? I know her face, I think.

MAN: Ah, yes. You might do. She's a famous actor now. She's called Lucy Wood. She can sing and dance very well and she usually works in the theatre.

[pause]

GIRL: Who's that other girl?

MAN: That's Katy. We were good friends at school, but I don't see her very often now. She was a nurse for many years and worked in a large hospital near here. But three or four years ago she left, and now she works at home. She looks after small children for parents who go out to work.

[pause]

GIRL: Who was your best friend?

MAN: This boy here. His name's Paul. He's a businessman now, and he's very rich. He makes and sells fridges. We play golf sometimes but I don't see him very often because he's so busy. He's always at his factory. He works all the time.

GIRL: Oh dear.

[pause]

Now listen to Part 3 again.

[The recording is repeated.]

[pause]

That is the end of Part 3.

[pause]

Part 4   *Listen and look. There is one example.*

[pause]

Which bird is the teacher thinking of?

[pause]

WOMAN: I'm thinking of a beautiful bird. Can you guess which bird?

BOY: Is it a parrot?

WOMAN: No. Let me help you. It swims on a lake like a duck but it has a longer neck and big strong wings.

BOY: Oh, I know. You're thinking of a swan!

WOMAN: That's right!

[pause]

Can you see the tick? Now you listen and tick the box.

[pause]

1 Which is Tom's picture?

WOMAN: Now. Let's look at the pictures that your class painted. Which is yours, Tom?

BOY: It's got a rocket in it.

WOMAN: Mm. Is it this one?

BOY: No. My picture has a planet, like that one, but mine's got stars in it, too.

[pause]

2 What is Tom going to paint today?

WOMAN: What would you like to paint today?

BOY: A tiger in the jungle?

WOMAN: Tom, you always choose that. Paint something different this time.

BOY: What about spiders on a leaf?

WOMAN: Or in a cave?

BOY: Yeah, that's better.

[pause]

3 What does Tom need next?

WOMAN: Have you finished with the scissors, Tom? Mary needs them.

BOY: Yes, I have. What's she doing?

WOMAN: She wants to cut some pictures out of a magazine.

BOY: Oh. Is there any more paper, Miss Rock? I need some for another picture.

WOMAN: Yes, there's some on my desk.

[pause]

4 What time does the football game start?

BOY: Our school team is going to play football with West End School at 4 o'clock, Miss. Are you going to watch us?

WOMAN: I'm not sure, Tom. This lesson finishes at 3.15. Then I have to tidy the classroom.

BOY: Oh, please, Miss Rock. It's an important game.

WOMAN: All right. But I can't stay until the end. I'll have to leave at 5.

[pause]

5 What are the new team clothes like?

BOY: Have you seen our new team clothes, Miss Rock?

WOMAN: Of course I have! White shorts and a red and black shirt.

BOY: No, Miss, it's different now. We wear black shorts and a red and white striped shirt.
WOMAN: What about socks?
BOY: They're white, like before.

[pause]

Now listen to Part 4 again.

[The recording is repeated.]

[pause]

That is the end of Part 4.

[pause]

Part 5 *Listen and look at the picture. There is one example.*

[pause]

MAN: Would you like to colour this picture?
GIRL: OK. Shall I colour the man whose foot is in the water?
MAN: Yes, all right. Colour his face blue.
GIRL: OK. That's the best colour for him, I think.

[pause]

Can you see the man's blue face? This is an example.
Now you listen and colour and write and draw.

[pause]

1

MAN: Now can you colour one of the snowmen?
GIRL: Which one? The one between the trees?
MAN: No, the big one at the front.
GIRL: OK. Can I colour it yellow?
MAN: Yes, that's fine.

[pause]

2

GIRL: Look – they're throwing snowballs.
MAN: Would you like to colour one of those children?
GIRL: Yes. Can I colour the one next to the skis?
MAN: All right. Colour his trousers brown.

[pause]

3

MAN: I'd like you to write something now. Can you see the man in the fur hat?
GIRL: Yes, he's pointing at a board.
MAN: Right. Under the word 'THIN' I'd like you to write the word 'ICE'. OK?
GIRL: OK. I've written it.

[pause]

4

GIRL: Can I draw something now?
MAN: Yes, of course. Look at the mountain.

GIRL: Which one? The one which is further away?
MAN: That's right. It looks smaller. Draw a house on the top of it and colour it purple.
GIRL: All right.

[pause]

5

MAN: Now, can you see those two girls with bikes?
GIRL: Yes, I can. Shall I colour the one who's pushing her bike?
MAN: No, colour the other one. The one who's riding over the bridge.
GIRL: All right. Can I colour her jacket green?
MAN: Yes, that's fine. You've finished now. Well done!

[pause]

Now listen to Part 5 again.

[The recording is repeated.]

[pause]

That is the end of the Flyers Practice Listening Test 1.

Reading and Writing

Part 1 (10 marks)
1 insects   2 salad   3 gloves   4 an octopus
5 a sledge   6 a ruler   7 winter   8 sugar
9 a stamp   10 jam

Part 2 (7 marks)
1 no   2 no   3 no   4 no   5 yes
6 yes   7 yes

Part 3 (5 marks)
1 E   2 G   3 A   4 H   5 B

Part 4 (6 marks)
1 storm   2 taxi   3 letters   4 thought
5 met   6 Dad's missing bag

Part 5 (7 marks)
1 her (bed)room   2 (Her/Katy's) mum/mother
3 piano   4 Whisper a Word   5 lights
6 brother   7 (new) guitar

Part 6 (10 marks)
1 not   2 their   3 found   4 drew   5 small
6 that   7 anything   8 to   9 of   10 because

Part 7 (5 marks)
1 In   2 was   3 of   4 said/shouted   5 be

Speaking

Part	Examiner does this:	Examiner says this:	Minimum response expected from child:	Back-up questions:
	Usher brings candidate in.	Usher to examiner: **Hello. This is (child's name*).** Examiner: **Hello, *. My name's** *Jane/Ms Smith.* **What's your surname?** **How old are you, *?**	Hello. *Silver* *ten*	**What's your family name?** **Are you** *ten*?
1	Shows candidate both **Find the Differences** pictures. Points to the trees in each picture. Describes things without pointing.	**Now, here are two pictures. My picture is nearly the same as yours, but some things are different. For example, in my picture there are four trees, but in your picture there are three trees. OK?** **I'm going to say something about my picture. You tell me how your picture is different.** **In my picture, there's a woman with a hat. She's sitting down.** **In my picture, I can see a truck near the castle.** **In my picture, the blue boat has got a red stripe.** **In my picture, the boy's wearing a scarf.** **In my picture, there's a plane on the left.** **In my picture, the old man in the green boat has caught a fish.**	*In my picture, the woman with the hat is standing.* *In my picture, I can see a motorbike near the castle.* *In my picture, the blue boat has a white stripe.* *In my picture, the boy isn't wearing a scarf.* *In my picture, the plane is on the right.* *In my picture, the old man has caught a shoe.*	1. Point at relevant difference/s. 2. Repeat statement. 3. Ask back-up question. **Is the woman sitting?** **Is there a truck near the castle?** **What colour is the stripe on the boat?** **Is the boy wearing a scarf?** **Is the plane on the left?** **Has the old man caught a fish?**
2	Shows candidate both **baby cousin** information pages. Then points to candidate's information page. Points to baby on the left on candidate's information page. Asks the questions. Points to baby on the right on candidate's information page.	**Daisy and Jack have both got a baby cousin. I don't know anything about Daisy's cousin, but you do. So I'm going to ask you some questions.** **What's Daisy's cousin's name?** **What colour are his eyes?** **How old is he?** **Where does he sleep?** **What's his favourite toy?** **Now you don't know anything about Jack's cousin, so you ask me some questions.**	*(It's) Robert* *(They're) grey.* *six months* *(in his) sister's bedroom* *(a) bear*	Point at the information if necessary.

* Remember to use the child's name throughout the test.

Part	Examiner does this:	Examiner says this:	Minimum response expected from child:	Back-up questions:
	Responds using information on examiner's information page.	Her name is Helen. She's five weeks old. They're brown. It's a duck. in her parents' bedroom	*What's her name? How old is she? What colour are her eyes? What's her favourite toy? Where does she sleep?*	Point at information cues if necessary.
3	Shows candidate **Picture Story** card. Allows time to look at the pictures.	These pictures tell a story. It's called 'A night at a hotel'. Just look at the pictures first.		
		Alex and Michael want to go camping. Mum's taking them to the mountains. They've got their tent in the car.		1. Point at the pictures. 2. Ask questions about the pictures.
		Now you tell the story.	*The tent's near a river. Alex and Michael are fishing and Mum's cooking lunch. It's sunny.*	**Where are they? What are the children doing? What's Mum doing? Is it sunny now?**
			It's raining now. They're all inside the tent. They're not happy.	**Where are they now?**
			It's night and it's still raining. Mum's driving to a hotel.	**Is it still raining? Where's Mum driving?**
			Now they are in a hotel bedroom. Alex, Michael and Mum are watching TV. They're happy.	**Where are they now? What are they doing? Are they happy?**
4	Puts the pictures away and turns to the candidate.	**Now, let's talk about your morning.**		
		What time do you get up?	*(at) 7 o'clock*	**Do you get up at 7 o'clock?**
		What do you have for breakfast?	*bread*	**Do you have *bread*?**
		Who do you eat breakfast with?	*my family*	**Do you eat breakfast with *your family*?**
		How do you go to school?	*(by) car*	**Do you go to school by car?**
		Tell me more about your morning.	*My first lesson is maths. I sit next to my friend. I have lunch at school.*	**What's your first lesson? Who do you sit next to? Where do you have *lunch*?**
		OK, thank you, *. Goodbye.	**Goodbye.**	

* Remember to use the child's name throughout the test.

Test 2 Answers

Listening

Part 1 *(5 marks)*
Lines should be drawn between:
1 Robert and the man holding the umbrella and the big bag
2 Michael and the boy reading a comic in the car
3 Katy and the girl looking for a scarf in a rucksack
4 Helen and the girl running up a hill with a dog
5 Emma and the girl putting on a coat, wearing a yellow hat

Part 2 *(5 marks)*
1 at/in a factory   2 train   3 7.30/seven thirty/half past seven
4 cakes   5 (a) uniform

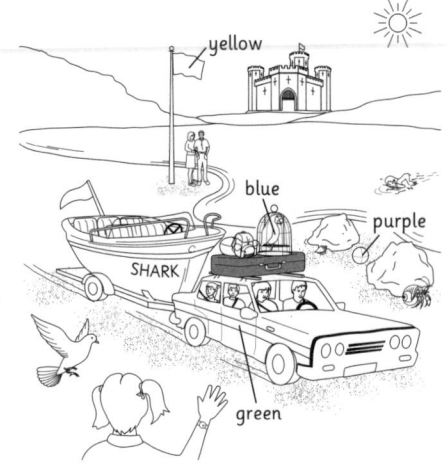

Part 3 *(5 marks)*
1 letter – D – behind computer   2 white gloves – E – on shelf
3 ring – G – under leaves   4 glasses – H – in fridge
5 keys – C – in jacket pocket

Part 4 *(5 marks)*
1 B   2 A   3 C   4 C   5 A

Part 5 *(5 marks)*
1 Colour the flag next to the sea – yellow
2 Write 'SHARK' on the boat
3 Draw a ball between the rocks and colour it – purple
4 Colour the stripe on the car – green
5 Colour the bird in the cage – blue

TRANSCRIPT   *Hello. This is the Cambridge Flyers Practice Listening Test, Test 2.*

Part 1   *Listen and look. There is one example.*

[pause]

GIRL: Look! This is a picture I took when we went camping!
MAN: What terrible weather!
GIRL: Yes, but we had a lot of fun. But look at Sarah ... she doesn't look very happy here.
MAN: Is that her? The girl who's holding the tent?
GIRL: Yes.

[pause]

Can you see the line? This is an example. Now you listen and draw lines.

[pause]

1

MAN: Who's the person with the umbrella and the big bag?
GIRL: Oh, that's my uncle. His name's Robert.
MAN: Did he drive you there?
GIRL: Yes. It was a nice, sunny day when we all left home!

[pause]

2

MAN: Weren't you afraid in the storm?
GIRL: No, I wasn't. But Michael was. He didn't want to come outside. Can you see him?
MAN: Oh, yes. What's he doing?
GIRL: He's reading his comic, I think.

[pause]

3

MAN: And who's that? You can't see her face very well.

GIRL: The person by the trees?

MAN: Not her ... the girl with the rucksack. What's she doing?

GIRL: Oh, you mean Katy! I think she's looking for her scarf.

[pause]

4

GIRL: And there's my sister.

MAN: Which one's she?

GIRL: The girl who's running up the hill. Her name's Helen. She's with our dog.

MAN: Oh, yes. I can see her.

GIRL: And that's her friend with the kite.

MAN: Uhuh.

[pause]

5

MAN: And who's the person who's putting her coat on?

GIRL: That's Emma. She's my cousin.

MAN: She looks like you!

GIRL: Yes, everyone says that. And I've got a yellow hat just like hers too.

MAN: Well, in that storm, you needed them, I think!

GIRL: Yes, we did!

[pause]

Now listen to Part 1 again.

[The recording is repeated.]

[pause]

That is the end of Part 1.

[pause]

Part 2 *Listen and look. There is one example.*

[pause]

BOY: Aunt Lucy, I have to do some homework about different jobs.

WOMAN: Do you? Well, you can write about my job!

BOY: OK. You're a cook, aren't you?

WOMAN: That's right. I love my job.

[pause]

Can you see the answer? Now you listen and write.

[pause]

BOY: I have to ask you five questions about your job.

WOMAN: OK. What's the first one?

BOY: Where do you work, Aunt Lucy?

WOMAN: I work at a factory.

BOY: OK. I have to write down the answers.

WOMAN: That's OK.

BOY: And how do you go to work? Do you go on the bus?

WOMAN: I can't do that. It takes too long so I go on the train.

BOY: OK. And what time do you have to start work every day?

WOMAN: Oh, very early! I start at half past seven, but I have to leave home at seven o'clock.

BOY: That IS early! And what do you make at the place where you work?

WOMAN: We make cakes.

BOY: Wow! What a great job! Do you eat some of them?

WOMAN: No! If you make them all day, you don't want to eat them!

BOY: And my last question. What do you have to wear there?

WOMAN: We all have to wear a uniform. I like it. It looks nice, too.

BOY: Good. Well, thanks for answering my questions. Can I come and visit you at work one day?

WOMAN: I don't know. Perhaps.

[pause]

Now listen to Part 2 again.

[The recording is repeated.]

[pause]

That is the end of Part 2.

[pause]

Part 3 *Listen and look. There is one example.*

[pause]

Betty's grandfather is always losing things! Where did he find each thing?

[pause]

GIRL: Why do you always lose things, Grandpa?

MAN: Because I have too many things and because I put them somewhere and then I forget where I put them, Betty! I couldn't find my nice new torch the other day – the one which you gave me. But when I played golf, I found it in my bag.

[pause]

Can you see the letter B? Now you listen and write a letter in each box.

[pause]

GIRL: Have you ever lost anything that was very important?

MAN: Oh, yes. About three months ago, I lost a very old letter. It was very important to me because Grandma wrote it to me 40 years ago! I was very sad when I couldn't find it. But then I found it behind the computer in the dining room so it was all right.

[pause]

GIRL: I lose a lot of things too.
MAN: We all do. When I was a policeman, I lost my white policeman's gloves one day. About a year later, I was standing on a chair. I was looking for something else on a high shelf when I found them!
GIRL: That was good!

[pause]

MAN: And another time, I lost my ring. The gold one which I wear sometimes.
GIRL: I know ...
MAN: Well, I took it off to wash the dog outside in the garden, then couldn't find it again. It was too dark to see very well. The next day I looked for it again. It was under some leaves. I was happy to find it!

[pause]

MAN: I lost my glasses too one day last week but I found them in the evening. I wanted a drink and opened the door of the fridge and there they were ... inside! It was good to find them. I put them on and watched television after that.

[pause]

GIRL: Grandpa! You are funny!
MAN: It's not always funny, Betty. One day, I couldn't find the keys to my car. I looked everywhere for them. In the end I decided to go to the shops on the bus! But they were in my jacket pocket all the time!

[pause]

Now listen to Part 3 again.

[The recording is repeated.]

[pause]

That is the end of Part 3.

[pause]

Part 4   *Listen and look. There is one example.*

[pause]

What game did Richard play today?

[pause]

WOMAN: Hello, Richard! How was your volleyball game? Did you win?
BOY: We did win, but not at that game! We played football this afternoon, remember?
WOMAN: Sorry! And tomorrow you're going to play basketball. Is that right?
BOY: Yes, Mum! And we'll win that game too, I think!

[pause]

Can you see the tick? Now you listen and tick the box.

[pause]

1 What has Richard hurt?

BOY: I played very well, but I fell over someone's leg in the second part.
WOMAN: You didn't hurt your foot again, like last time?
BOY: No, but I put my hand out on the ground when I fell, and someone stood on it.
WOMAN: Oh dear. Is it OK now?
BOY: Yes.

[pause]

2 Where are Richard's football shorts?

BOY: Can you wash all my football things for me, Mum? I'll need them again very soon.
WOMAN: Yes, put them on the kitchen floor and I'll wash them in a minute.
BOY: OK ... here's my towel. Oh! But where are my football shorts? They aren't on the balcony, are they, with the other wet things?
WOMAN: No. Is that them over there? By the door?
BOY: Oh, yes!

[pause]

3 What does Richard need for football?

WOMAN: This football shirt is too small for you now, isn't it, Richard?
BOY: No, it's OK. I like it like that, but I'd like a new sweater to wear at football games.
WOMAN: OK, and what about some new football socks? Do you need some bigger ones yet?
BOY: I don't think so. No, my old ones are fine, thanks.

[pause]

4 What is Richard going to do on Friday evening?

BOY: My next football game is on Friday evening, I think ...
WOMAN: But you're going to go to your friend's party that evening, aren't you?
BOY: Oh, yes! You're right! I forgot about that. And the next evening, Dad's going to take me to the cinema, he said. Are you going to come?
WOMAN: Of course! It's a film that I want to see too.
BOY: Great!

[pause]

5 What's Richard going to do first?

BOY: So, can I have something to eat now, Mum? I'm very hungry.
WOMAN: No, go and have a shower, Richard. You can eat after that.
BOY: OK. And where are my clean jeans? Do you know?
WOMAN: They're in your room ... which is very untidy, Richard! You must go and tidy it later.
BOY: OK.

[pause]

Now listen to Part 4 again.

[The recording is repeated.]

[pause]

That is the end of Part 4.

[pause]

Part 5 *Listen and look at the picture.*
There is one example.

[pause]

MAN:	Shall we look at this picture now?
GIRL:	Yes. Is it a family on holiday?
MAN:	Yes. Look at all their things!
GIRL:	Can I colour something?
MAN:	Yes, please. Colour the big suitcase orange. Can you see it?
GIRL:	Yes. OK, I'm doing that now.

[pause]

Can you see the orange suitcase? This is an example.
Now you listen and colour and write and draw.

[pause]

1

GIRL:	Now what else can I colour? How about the flag?
MAN:	Yes! Good idea! Colour the one which is next to the people, next to the sea.
GIRL:	OK. But can I choose the colour?
MAN:	Yes, you can.
GIRL:	I'll use yellow then.
MAN:	All right.

[pause]

2

MAN:	Would you like to write something on this picture too?
GIRL:	Oh, yes. I like writing. What can I write?
MAN:	The boat hasn't got a name. Let's give it one.
GIRL:	OK. What can I call it?
MAN:	Write 'SHARK' on it. That's a good name.
GIRL:	All right. I'll do that now.

[pause]

3

GIRL:	And can I draw something in this picture too?
MAN:	Yes. Draw a ball between the two rocks. Can you do that?
GIRL:	Yes, that's easy. And then can I colour it?
MAN:	Yes. Make it purple. I love that colour.
GIRL:	Me too!
MAN:	Good.

[pause]

4

MAN:	Look at the car that is pulling the boat.
GIRL:	Can I colour the stripe on the boat?
MAN:	No, colour the stripe on the car.
GIRL:	OK. Can I make it green?
MAN:	Oh, OK, yes, you can.
GIRL:	Thanks.

[pause]

5

MAN:	Now, we need to colour one more thing.
GIRL:	How about the bird? The one in the cage?
MAN:	All right. Let's make it pink.
GIRL:	Can I colour it blue? We haven't used that colour yet.
MAN:	Yes. If you prefer that colour, that's fine.
GIRL:	Great! I've finished.
MAN:	Well done!

[pause]

Now listen to Part 5 again.

[The recording is repeated.]

[pause]

That is the end of the Flyers Practice Listening Test 2.

Reading and Writing

Part 1 (10 marks)

1 jam 2 flour 3 paper 4 dinosaurs
5 gold 6 an octopus 7 glass 8 salad
9 insects 10 biscuits

Part 2 (7 marks)

1 no 2 yes 3 no 4 no 5 no 6 no 7 yes

Part 3 (5 marks)

1 F 2 E 3 G 4 D 5 A

Part 4 (6 marks)

1 left 2 sad 3 emails 4 doctor 5 waiting
6 Tom breaks his arm

Part 5 (7 marks)

1 (favourite) doll/dolly 2 (some) lemonade
3 (dark) forest 4 (high) rocks 5 snow
6 cried 7 (had) found

Part 6 (10 marks)

1 every 2 another 3 enjoy 4 by 5 who
6 can 7 than 8 work 9 they 10 also

Part 7 (5 marks)

1 animals/creatures/species 2 There 3 take/get
4 are 5 does

Speaking

Part	Examiner does this:	Examiner says this:	Minimum response expected from child:	Back-up questions:
	Usher brings candidate in.	Usher to examiner: **Hello. This is (child's name*).** Examiner: **Hello, *. My name's** *Jane/Ms Smith.* **What's your surname?** **How old are you, *?**	Hello. *Silver* *ten*	What's your family name? Are you *ten*?
1	Shows candidate both **Find the Differences** pictures. Points to the dog in each picture. Describes things without pointing.	**Now, here are two pictures. My picture is nearly the same as yours, but some things are different.** **For example, in my picture the dog is black, but in your picture it's white. OK?** **I'm going to say something about my picture. You tell me how your picture is different.** **In my picture, it's sunny.** **In my picture, the woman in the pink skirt is standing.** **In my picture, the red suitcase is bigger than the blue one.** **In my picture, four people are walking to the plane.** **In my picture, the magazine on the table is open.** **In my picture, a man's buying a drink. He's wearing a shirt with spots.**	 *In my picture, it's cloudy.* *In my picture, the woman's sitting down.* *In my picture, the red suitcase is smaller.* *In my picture, three people are walking to the plane.* *In my picture, it's closed.* *In my picture, he's wearing a shirt with stripes.*	 1. Point at relevant difference/s. 2. Repeat statement. 3. Ask back-up question. Is it sunny? Is the woman standing? Which suitcase is bigger? How many people are walking to the plane? Is the magazine open? Is the man wearing a shirt with spots?
2	Shows candidate both **birthday party** information pages. Then points to candidate's information page. Points to girl on candidate's information page. Asks the questions.	**Jill and Paul are friends. They had birthday parties last week. I don't know anything about Jill's party, but you do. So I'm going to ask you some questions.** **Which day was Jill's party?** **How many friends did she invite?** **What did they eat?** **Where was the party?** **What was Jill's favourite present?**	 *Saturday* *ten* *cake* *(at) her house* *(a) scarf*	 Point at the information if necessary.

* Remember to use the child's name throughout the test.

Part	Examiner does this:	Examiner says this:	Minimum response expected from child:	Back-up questions:
	Points to boy on candidate's information page. Responds using information on examiner's information page.	**Now you don't know anything about Paul's party, so you ask me some questions.** **a computer game** **in the park** **pizza** **Wednesday** **12**	*What was Paul's favourite present?* *Where was the party?* *What did they eat?* *Which day was Paul's party?* *How many friends did he invite?*	Point at information cues if necessary.
3	Shows candidate **Picture Story** card. Allows time to look at the pictures.	**These pictures tell a story. It's called 'Katy's new football clothes'. Just look at the pictures first.** **Katy's brother is playing football. Katy can't play with him because she hasn't got any football clothes. She's sad.** **Now you tell the story.**	*Katy's asleep in bed. In her dream, she's playing football.* *Katy's mother is making a shirt.* *Katy's mother has made some football clothes. Katy's very surprised.* *Now Katy can play football with her brother. She's very happy.*	1. Point at the pictures. 2. Ask questions about the pictures. Where's Katy now? What's she doing in her dream? What is Katy's mother doing? What has Katy's mother made? Is Katy surprised? What can Katy do now? How's she feeling?
4	Puts the pictures away and turns to the candidate.	**Now, let's talk about meals and food in your house.** **What's your favourite food?** **What food don't you like eating?** **Who cooks in your house?** **What do you eat for your lunch on Sunday******?** **Tell me about breakfast in your house.**	*chips/fries* *onions* *(my) mum* *chicken* *We have breakfast at 7 o'clock.* *We eat in the kitchen.* *We eat bread and fruit.*	Do you like *chips/fries*? Do you like *onions*? Does *your mother* cook the meals? Do you eat *chicken* for lunch on Sunday**? What time do you have breakfast? Where do you eat? What do you have for breakfast?
		OK, thank you, *. **Goodbye.**	Goodbye.	

* Remember to use the child's name throughout the test.

** Or substitute another day that is appropriate to your country.

Test 3 Answers

Listening

Part 1 (5 marks)
Lines should be drawn between:
1 David and the boy reading a comic on the sofa
2 Harry and the boy fishing in the river outside, wearing a hat
3 Sarah and the girl lying on the floor, looking at pictures
4 Daisy and the girl playing on the computer, by the present and the shoes
5 Betty and the woman wearing glasses, standing

Part 2 (5 marks)
1 June   2 Burley (correct spelling)   3 10/ten (children)
4 (a) rucksack   5 insects

Part 3 (5 marks)
1 pizzas – G – factory   2 vegetables – E – flats
3 flour – A – museum   4 chocolates – B – airport
5 jam – F – chemist's

Part 4 (5 marks)
1 B   2 B   3 A   4 B   5 C

Part 5 (5 marks)
1 Colour the coat of the woman at the bus stop – orange
2 Colour the bigger swan – yellow
3 Draw a cloud above the tree and colour the cloud – blue
4 Write 'HILL' above 'STREET'
5 Colour the pilot's suitcase – brown

TRANSCRIPT   *Hello. This is the Cambridge Flyers Practice Listening Test, Test 3.*

Part 1   *Listen and look. There is one example.*

[pause]

GIRL: This is a picture that I took at my friend's house. She lives in another country. I went to visit her there in the summer holidays.
MAN: Which one's your friend?
GIRL: Jane. The girl who's playing the piano. She's got dark hair.
MAN: Oh, yes. Is she good at music?
GIRL: Yes. She's a great singer too.

[pause]

Can you see the line? This is an example. Now you listen and draw lines.

[pause]

1

MAN: Who's the boy on the sofa, there, next to the television?
GIRL: That's my friend's cousin. His name's David.
MAN: What's he reading? It's funny, I think.
GIRL: Oh, it's just one of his comics. He's got lots of them.

[pause]

2

MAN: I can see out of the doors. Is that a lake in their garden?

GIRL: No, it's a river. Can you see Harry? The boy who's fishing there.

MAN: Which one are you talking about? The one who's wearing shorts?

GIRL: Not him, the one with the hat.

MAN: Oh, yes. I see now.

[pause]

3

MAN: And the girl who's lying on the floor, who's that?

GIRL: Oh, that's Sarah. She doesn't like sitting on chairs!

MAN: What's she playing with? I can't see very well.

GIRL: She's not playing. She's looking at some pictures of her friends.

MAN: Oh.

[pause]

4

MAN: There are lots of children in your friend's family!

GIRL: Oh, they're not all her brothers and sisters. Can you see the girl who's playing on the computer?

MAN: Yes.

GIRL: Well, she lives in the house next to my friend's. Her name's Daisy. It was her birthday when I was there. You can see one of her presents by her shoes. Look!

MAN: Oh, yes.

[pause]

5

GIRL: And there's my friend's mother, Betty. She's very kind.

MAN: The woman who's turning on the lamp?

GIRL: No, the woman who's standing next to her – the one who's wearing the glasses. She often loses them. She takes them off and can't remember where she put them!

MAN: Oh dear!

[pause]

Now listen to Part 1 again.

[The recording is repeated.]

[pause]

That is the end of Part 1.

[pause]

Part 2   *Listen and look. There is one example.*

[pause]

BOY: Mum! Miss Right at school is going to take some of us on a camping holiday! Can I go?

WOMAN: For how long?

BOY: It's just for three days!

WOMAN: Oh! I see.

[pause]

Can you see the answer? Now you listen and write.

[pause]

WOMAN: When is this holiday?

BOY: She's going to leave on June 6th and come back home on the 9th.

WOMAN: Hmm. I must write that in my diary. All right. And where will you camp?

BOY: On a farm. It's called Burley Farm. That's B-U-R-L-E-Y. Miss Right wrote it on the board.

WOMAN: Oh, I know. It's near the forest. We went there on holiday once. Do you remember?

BOY: No!

WOMAN: You were very little. But I have a few more questions.

BOY: OK.

WOMAN: How many children are going to go?

BOY: Only ten children and there will be two teachers with us. That's OK, isn't it?

WOMAN: Yes. What do you have to take with you?

BOY: We don't need to take any tents. The teachers will bring them, but I will have to take a rucksack to carry things in.

WOMAN: OK, and what are you going to do on this holiday? Sports? Learn about the farm animals there?

BOY: No. We're going to learn about insects. We're going to watch them, draw them and take pictures of them.

WOMAN: That sounds interesting! Perhaps I'll come too!

BOY: Mum! You can't! You're too big!

[pause]

Now listen to Part 2 again.

[The recording is repeated.]

[pause]

That is the end of Part 2.

[pause]

Part 3 Listen and look. There is one
example.

[pause]

*Fred works in the town. He has to
take food to different places in the
town. Where does he take each thing?*

[pause]

WOMAN: Fred, is the truck outside? You've got all
this food to take today.

MAN: Yes. I'm going to leave in a minute. I'll
take these biscuits to the circus first. It's
not far away. Perhaps I'll see some lions
and tigers there!

[pause]

*Can you see the letter D? Now you
listen and write a letter in each box.*

[pause]

WOMAN: Drive very carefully. There's a lot of traffic
today.

MAN: I know. I'll take that box of pizzas next …
but where must I take it? Oh, I remember!
They're for the man who works at the
factory – the one in Salt Street. Where is
that?

WOMAN: The map's in the back of the truck.

MAN: OK.

[pause]

MAN: And then I'll take these vegetables to
Mrs Cook. She lives in an apartment on
that busy corner in town. You know, the
one opposite the hospital. I'll have to
carry them up a lot of stairs. The lift there
doesn't work!

WOMAN: Oh dear!

[pause]

WOMAN: And where must you take this? Have you
written all this down?

MAN: Yes! The big bag of flour? Oh, that's for
Mr Card at the old science museum. He
likes making bread so he uses a lot of it
each month. He phoned me yesterday.
He said he needs it this afternoon. Can
you make bread, Lucy?

WOMAN: No, I've never tried. I just buy mine.

[pause]

MAN: Now who's this for?

WOMAN: What?

MAN: This big box of chocolates! Someone's
going to be very happy to get this. Oh,
here's the address … I've got to take it
to the airport. Oh dear! That's a long way
away. Well, I can have my lunch there too
in the restaurant.

WOMAN: That's a good idea, Fred.

[pause]

WOMAN: And here's the last box.

MAN: Oh, yes, the pineapple jam. I mustn't
drop that. The glass will break and it took
hours to make it. That's for Mrs Hide at
the chemist's. It's her favourite so she
buys a lot of it. Now, is there anything
else to take today, Lucy?

WOMAN: No, that's everything.

MAN: Good!

[pause]

Now listen to Part 3 again.

[The recording is repeated.]

[pause]

That is the end of Part 3.

[pause]

Part 4 Listen and look. There is one
example.

[pause]

*Where does Jack want to go on his
birthday?*

[pause]

WOMAN: Jack! Would you like to have a picnic on
your birthday, in the countryside?

BOY: That's a great idea, Mum, but it might be
a cold day. Can we go to the cinema and
see a film? I'd like to do that.

WOMAN: All right. Or you can go to the sports
centre that day with your friends.

BOY: No, I don't want to have my party there.

[pause]

*Can you see the tick? Now you listen
and tick the box.*

[pause]

1 Which film do they choose?

BOY: There are lots of great films to see this
week. It's difficult to choose.

WOMAN: I'd like to see the one about rockets in
space! That sounds exciting.

BOY: Oh, no. I think the one about the big fire
and all the firemen is better.

WOMAN: But some of your friends might be afraid.
There's one about the dinosaurs. What
do you think?

BOY: Yes. That's the best idea.

[pause]

2 When will Jack see the film?

BOY: Can we go on Monday after school?
That's the day of my birthday so I'd like
that the best.

WOMAN: That will be difficult because Dad's got to work that evening. Let's have a small party at home that day. We can see your film the day before that, on Sunday, if you like.

BOY: OK. And can I invite some friends here on Saturday, too?

WOMAN: I'm not sure. I'll ask Dad first. I think we're going to go out that afternoon.

BOY: OK.

[pause]

3 What time must Jack's friends come to his house?

BOY: I'll tell my friends at school tomorrow to come to my house first. What time should they arrive here?

WOMAN: Well, let's look in the newspaper to find out about the film first. Here it is! It starts at a quarter past five.

BOY: So, shall I tell them to come at quarter to five?

WOMAN: Let's say half past four because it'll take us about thirty-five minutes to get there.

BOY: All right.

[pause]

4 How will they buy the cinema tickets?

BOY: You can get cinema tickets on the computer now, Mum. Did you know that?

WOMAN: No, I didn't know that! Wow! That's good. But I'll phone the cinema to buy them this time. I want to speak to the woman there.

BOY: OK. Or we can buy the tickets at the cinema. There won't be too many people there, will there?

WOMAN: I don't want to do that, Jack.

[pause]

5 How will they get to the cinema?

BOY: Are we going to walk to the cinema like last time?

WOMAN: Ermm ... I think it's too far. You were tired, remember? But there are too many of us to drive there in Dad's car.

BOY: Well, in a big taxi, then?

WOMAN: Well, that's quite expensive, but OK, we'll do that.

BOY: It's going to be fun. I love birthdays!

[pause]

Now listen to Part 4 again.

[The recording is repeated.]

[pause]

That is the end of Part 4.

[pause]

Part 5   *Listen and look at the picture. There is one example.*

[pause]

MAN: Let's colour this picture now, shall we? Look at the rainbow!

GIRL: Oh, yes. And there's lots of rain on the ground. The people are very wet!

MAN: That's right! Look at the umbrella in the air. The wind is very strong! Can you colour it green for me?

GIRL: Yes. I can do that. It's easy.

[pause]

Can you see the green umbrella? This is an example. Now you listen and colour and draw and write.

[pause]

1

GIRL: What can I colour now? One of the people who are waiting for the bus?

MAN: Ermm ... OK. Can you see the woman who's standing there? She's holding the child's hand.

GIRL: Yes. Can I colour her coat?

MAN: Yes, all right! Make it orange.

GIRL: OK.

[pause]

2

GIRL: Are those swans on the grass?

MAN: Yes. I think they're waiting to cross the road. Colour the bigger one. The one with the longer neck, on the left.

GIRL: Can I make it pink?

MAN: Ermm ... no, let's colour it yellow.

GIRL: All right. I like that colour too. They've got big wings, haven't they?

MAN: Yes.

[pause]

3

MAN: Would you like to draw something here?

GIRL: In this picture? Now?

MAN: Yes! Can you draw a little cloud in the sky? Draw it there, just above the tree.

GIRL: OK. I can put one there. Shall I colour it, too?

MAN: Yes! Good idea! Colour it blue. That will look good.

GIRL: All right. I've got that colour. I'll do that now.

MAN: Thank you.

[pause]

4

MAN: And can you write something here, too? I'd like this road to have a name.

GIRL: OK. I can see the word 'STREET' on the little low wall next to the shop. Shall I write it there?

MAN: Yes. Write the word 'HILL' above that.

GIRL: All right. I can spell that word.

MAN: Good. Well done!

[pause]

5

GIRL: Look at that man. Is he a pilot?

MAN: Perhaps. I don't know.

GIRL: Well, can I colour his uniform?

MAN: No, but you can colour his suitcase if you like. It looks very heavy.

GIRL: It does. You're right! Shall I make it brown?

MAN: Yes. That looks great now. Thank you.

[pause]

Now listen to Part 5 again.

[The recording is repeated.]

[pause]

That is the end of the Flyers Practice Listening Test 3.

Reading and Writing

Part 1 (10 marks)
1 an umbrella   2 a farmer   3 cookies
4 soap   5 a comb   6 an octopus
7 a flashlight   8 bats   9 doctors   10 plates

Part 2 (7 marks)
1 no 2 no 3 yes 4 no 5 no 6 no 7 yes

Part 3 (5 marks)
1 F   2 B   3 G   4 H   5 C

Part 4 (6 marks)
1 top   2 afraid   3 tent   4 gold   5 forget
6 My very best three days

Part 5 (7 marks)
1 dark   2 silver   3 unhappy/sad   4 school/class
5 (the) birds   6 (lovely) (red) (spotted) butterfly
7 the (small) leaf/a leaf

Part 6 (10 marks)
1 ago   2 that   3 Since   4 can't   5 of
6 all   7 moves   8 sing   9 No   10 in

Part 7 (5 marks)
1 fell/tripped/slipped   2 on/across/over
3 socks   4 from/at   5 were/felt/got

Speaking

Part	Examiner does this:	Examiner says this:	Minimum response expected from child:	Back-up questions:
	Usher brings candidate in.	Usher to examiner: **Hello. This is (child's name*).**		
		Examiner: **Hello, *. My name's** *Jane/Ms Smith.*	**Hello.**	
		What's your surname?	*Silver*	**What's your family name?**
		How old are you, *?	*ten*	**Are you** *ten*?
1	Shows candidate both **Find the Differences** pictures. Points to the sky in each picture. Describes things without pointing.	**Now, here are two pictures. My picture is nearly the same as yours, but some things are different. For example, in my picture it's a sunny day, but in your picture it's cloudy. OK?** **I'm going to say something about my picture. You tell me how your picture is different.** **In my picture, there's a bicycle under a tree.** **In my picture, the flags are green and yellow.** **In my picture, there's a woman with brown hair. She's holding a fan.** **In my picture, I can see a rucksack next to the man's chair.** **In my picture, a girl has won the race.** **In my picture, a boy has fallen over. He's wearing shorts.**	*In my picture, there's a motorbike.* *In my picture, the flags are green and pink.* *In my picture, the woman's holding a hat.* *In my picture, I can't see a rucksack.* *In my picture, a boy has won the race.* *In my picture, the boy's wearing trousers.*	1. Point at relevant difference/s. 2. Repeat statement. 3. Ask back-up question. **Is there a bicycle under a tree?** **What colour are the flags?** **What's the woman holding?** **Can you see a rucksack next to the man's chair?** **Who has won the race?** **Is the boy wearing shorts?**
2	Shows candidate both **school** information pages. Then points to candidate's information page. Points to boy on candidate's information page. Asks the questions. Points to girl on candidate's information page.	**Tony and Vicky are cousins. They go to different schools. I don't know anything about Tony's school, but you do. So I'm going to ask you some questions.** **Is Tony's school new or old?** **How many children are there in the school?** **Is there a swimming pool?** **Where is the school?** **What time do classes start?** **Now you don't know anything about Vicky's school, so you ask me some questions.**	*new* *141* *yes* *(in) Castle Road* *(at) 8 o'clock*	Point at the information if necessary.

* Remember to use the child's name throughout the test.

Part	Examiner does this:	Examiner says this:	Minimum response expected from child:	Back-up questions:
	Responds using information on examiner's information page.	**It's in Hospital Road. There are 165.** **at 9 o'clock** **It's old.** **No, there isn't.**	*Where is Vicky's school?* *How many children are there in the school?* *What time do classes start?* *Is the school new or old?* *Is there a swimming pool?*	Point at information cues if necessary.
3	Shows candidate **Picture Story** card. Allows time to look at the pictures.	**These pictures tell a story. It's called 'Sarah meets her favourite singer'. Just look at the pictures first.** **Sarah's in her bedroom. She has lots of photos of Lucy Lake on the walls. Lucy Lake is a famous singer. Sarah's mum is saying, 'Let's go for a walk.'** **Now you tell the story.**		1. Point at the pictures. 2. Ask questions about the pictures.
			Sarah and her mum are walking in the park.	Where are Sarah and her mum?
			Sarah has seen Lucy Lake. She's walking with her dog.	Who has Sarah seen? What's Lucy Lake doing?
			Sarah's mum is taking a photo of Sarah with Lucy Lake.	What's Sarah's mum doing?
			Now there's one big photo in Sarah's bedroom.	How many photos are there in Sarah's bedroom now?
			It's a photo of Sarah and Lucy Lake together.	Who's in the photo?
4	Puts the pictures away and turns to the candidate.	**Now let's talk about clothes.** **What's your favourite colour?** **What do you wear to school?** **What clothes do you want to buy?** **What <u>don't</u> you like wearing?** **Tell me about a clothes shop that you like.**	*(It's) purple.* *(I wear) trousers and a shirt.* *(I want to buy) some shoes.* *(I don't like) hats.* *It's in the city.* *It's very big.* *I go there with my mum.*	Do you like *purple*? Do you wear a school uniform? Do you want to buy some *shoes*? Do you like wearing *hats*? Where is the clothes shop? Is it big or small? Who do you go there with?
		OK, thank you, *. **Goodbye.**	**Goodbye.**	

* Remember to use the child's name throughout the test.

COMBINED STARTERS, MOVERS AND FLYERS THEMATIC VOCABULARY LIST

For ease of reference, vocabulary is arranged in semantic groups or themes. Some words appear under more than one heading.

In addition to the topics, notions and concepts listed for the syllabus, the following categories appear:

- useful words and expressions
- adjectives
- determiners
- adverbs
- prepositions
- conjunctions
- pronouns
- verbs
- modals
- question words
- names

s – first appears at *Starters*

m – first appears at *Movers*

f – first appears at *Flyers*

ANIMALS

s	animal
m	bat
m	bear
s	bird
f	butterfly
m	cage
f	camel
s	cat
s	chicken
s	cow
s	crocodile
f	dinosaur
s	dog
m	dolphin
s	duck
s	elephant
s	fish (s & pl)
m	fly
s	frog
f	fur
s	giraffe
s	goat
s	hippo
s	horse
f	insect
m	kangaroo
m	kitten
m	lion
s	lizard
s	monkey
s	mouse/mice
f	octopus
m	panda
m	parrot
m	pet
m	puppy
m	rabbit
m	shark
s	sheep (s & pl)
s	snake
s	spider
f	swan
s	tail
s	tiger
m	whale
f	wing
s	zoo

THE BODY & FACE

s	arm
m	back
m	beard
m	blond(e)
s	body
m	curly
s	ear
s	eye
s	face
m	fair
s	foot/feet
s	hair
s	hand
s	head
s	leg
m	moustache
s	mouth
m	neck
s	nose
m	shoulder
s	smile
m	stomach
m	straight
m	tooth/teeth

CLOTHES

s	bag
f	belt
s	clothes
m	coat
s	dress
s	glasses
f	glove
s	handbag
s	hat
s	jacket
s	jeans
f	pocket
f	ring
m	scarf
s	shirt
s	shoe
f	shorts
s	skirt
s	sock
f	spot
f	spotted
f	stripe
f	striped
m	sweater
f	tights
s	trousers

s T-shirt
f umbrella
f uniform
s watch
s wear

COLOURS

s black
s blue
s brown
f gold
s green
s grey (or gray)
s orange
s pink
s purple
s red
f silver
s white
s yellow

FAMILY & FRIENDS

m aunt
s baby
s boy
s brother
s child/children
s cousin
s dad(dy)
m daughter
s family
s father
s friend
s girl
m granddaughter
s grandfather
s grandma
s grandmother
s grandpa
m grandparent
m grandson
m grown up
f husband
s live
s man/men
f married
s Miss
s mother
s Mr
s Mrs
s mum(my)
s old
m parent
s person/people
s sister
m son

f surname
s their
s them
s they
m uncle
s us
s we
f wife
s woman/women
s you
s young
s your

FOOD & DRINK

s apple
s banana
s bean
f biscuit (US cookie)
m bottle
m bowl
s bread
s breakfast
s burger
f butter
s cake
f candy (UK sweets)
s carrot
m cheese
s chicken
s chips (US fries)
f chocolate
f chopsticks
s coconut
m coffee
f cookie (UK biscuit)
m cup
s dinner
s drink (n & v)
s eat
s egg
s fish
f flour
s food
f fork
s fries (UK chips)
s fruit
m glass of
s grape
m hungry
s ice cream
f jam
s juice
f knife
s lemon
s lemonade
s lime
s lunch

s mango
f meal
s meat
s milk
s onion
s orange
m pasta
s pea
s pear
f pepper
m picnic
f piece
s pineapple
f pizza
f plate
s potato
s rice
m salad
f salt
m sandwich
s sausage
f smell
f snack
m soup
f spoon
f sugar
s supper
f sweets (US candy)
f taste
m tea
m thirsty
s tomato
m vegetable
s water
s watermelon

HEALTH

f chemist('s)
m cold
m cough
f dentist
m doctor
m earache
m fine
m headache
m hospital
m hurt
f ill
m matter (What's the matter?)
f medicine
m nurse
f problem
m stomach-ache
m temperature
m toothache

THE HOME

m address
s apartment
s armchair
m balcony
m basement
s bath
s bathroom
s bed
s bedroom
m blanket
s bookcase
s box
f brush
s camera
s chair
s clock
f comb
s computer
f cooker
s cupboard
s desk
f diary
s dining room
s doll
s door
m downstairs
m dream
m elevator
f envelope
m fan
s flat
s floor
s flower
f fridge
s garden
s hall
m home
s house
f key
s kitchen
s lamp
f letter
m lift
s living room
s mat
s mirror
f money
s painting
s phone
s picture
s radio
s room
f secret
f shelf
m shopping
m shower

s sleep
f soap
s sofa
m stairs
f stamp
f swing
s table
f telephone
s television/TV
f toilet
m toothbrush
m towel
s toy
s tree
m upstairs
s wall
m wash (n)
s watch
s window

MATERIALS

f card
f glass
f gold
f metal
f paper
f plastic
f silver
f wood
f wool

NUMBERS

s Cardinals: 1–20
m Cardinals: 21–100
f Cardinals: 101–1000
m Ordinals: 1st–20th
f Ordinals: 21st–31st

PLACES & DIRECTIONS

m above
f airport
m bank
s behind
s between
f bookshop
f bridge
m bus station
f bus stop
m café
f castle
f chemist('s)
m cinema
f circus
f club
f college

f corner
f east
f end
f factory
m farm
f fire station
f front
f get to
s here
m hospital
f hotel
s in
s in front of
f kilometre(s) (US) kilometer(s)
f left
m library
f London
m map
m market
f museum
s next to
f north
s on
f over
s park
m place
s playground
f police station
f post office
f restaurant
f right
m road
s shop (US store)
f south
m square
f station
s store (UK shop)
m straight
f straight on
s street
m supermarket
m swimming pool
f theatre
s there
s under
f university
f way
f west
s zoo

SCHOOL

s alphabet
s answer
f art
s ask
f bin

s board
s book
s bookcase
s class
s classroom
s close
f club
f college
s colour
f competition
s computer
s correct
s cross
s cupboard
s desk
f dictionary
s door
s draw(ing)
s English
s eraser
f exam (examination)
s example
s find
f flag
s floor
f geography
f glue
f group
f history
m homework
s know
f language
s learn
s lesson
s letter (as in alphabet)
s line
s listen (to)
s look
f maths
m mistake
s name
s number
s open
s page
s part
s pen
s pencil
s picture
s playground
s question
s read
s right (as in correct)
s rubber
f rucksack
s ruler
s school
f science
f scissors

s sentence
f shelf
s spell
s stand (up)
s story
f student
f subject
s teacher
s tell
s test (n & v)
m text
s tick (n & v)
s understand
f university
s wall
s window
s word
s write
f zero

SPORTS & LEISURE

s badminton
s ball
s baseball
s basketball
m bat
s beach
s bike
s boat
s book
s bounce
s camera
s catch
m CD
m comic/comic book
f conversation
f diary
s doll
s draw(ing)
s drive
f drum
m DVD
s enjoy
s favourite
m film
s fish(ing)
f flashlight
s fly
s football (US soccer)
s game
f golf
s guitar
s hit
s hobby
s hockey
m holiday
f hotel

s jump
s kick (n & v)
s kite
s listen (to)
f magazine
m movie
m music
s paint(ing)
m party
s photo
s piano
s picture
s play (with)
f player (as in CD player)
f postcard
m present
f programme (US program)
f pyramid
f race
s radio
s read
s ride (n & v)
f rucksack
s run
m sail
f score
s sing
m skate
f ski
f sledge
f snowball
f snowman
s soccer (UK football)
s song
s sport
m sports centre
s story
f suitcase
m swim (n)
m swimming pool
f swing
s table tennis
f tape recorder
f team
s television/TV
s tennis
f tent
s throw
f torch
m towel
s toy
s TV/television
f umbrella
m video
f volleyball
m walk (n)
s watch

TIME

f a.m.
m after
s afternoon
m age
f ago
m always
f autumn
m before
s birthday
f century
f Christmas
s clock
f date
s day
f early
s end
s evening
m every
f future
f half
f hour
f late
f later
f midday
f midnight
f minute
f month
s morning
m never
s night
f o'clock
f p.m.
f past
f quarter
m sometimes
f spring
f summer
f time
s today
f tomorrow
f tonight
s watch
m week
m weekend
f winter
f year
m yesterday
The days of the week:
m Sunday
m Monday
m Tuesday
m Wednesday
m Thursday
m Friday
m Saturday
The months of the year:

f January
f February
f March
f April
f May
f June
f July
f August
f September
f October
f November
f December

TOYS

s ball
s baseball
s basketball
s bike
s car
s doll
s football
s game
s helicopter
s kite
s lorry (US truck)
s monster
s plane
s robot
s toy
s train
m treasure
s truck (UK lorry)

TRANSPORT

f airport
f ambulance
f bicycle
s bike
s boat
s bus
m bus station
s car
m drive (n)
s drive (v)
m driver
f fire engine
s fly
s go
s helicopter
s lorry (US truck)
s motorbike
s plane
s ride (v)
m ride (n)
f rocket
s run
f station

s swim
f taxi
m ticket
f traffic
s train
s truck (UK lorry)
s walk

WEATHER

m cloud
m cloudy
f fog
f foggy
f ice
m rain
m rainbow
f sky
m snow
f storm
s sun
m sunny
m weather
m wind
m windy

WORK

f actor/actress
f airport
f ambulance
f artist
f astronaut
f business
f businessman/woman
f circus
m clown
f cook
f dentist
m doctor
f engineer
f factory
m farmer
f fireman/woman
f footballer
m hospital
f job
f journalist
f mechanic
f meeting
f news
f newspaper
m nurse
f office
f painter
f photographer
f pilot
m pirate
f police station

f	policeman/woman			m	difficult	f	metal
f	queen			s	dirty	f	missing
f	secretary			s	double	m	more
f	singer			f	dry	m	most
s	teacher			f	each	s	my
f	tennis player			f	early	m	naughty
f	waiter			m	easy	s	new
m	work			f	empty	f	next

THE WORLD AROUND US

USEFUL WORDS & EXPRESSIONS

s	bye (-bye)
m	come on!
f	excellent
m	excuse me
s	goodbye
s	hello
s	I don't know
s	no
s	oh
s	oh dear
s	OK
s	pardon
s	please
s	right
m	see you!
s	so
s	sorry
s	thank you
s	thanks
s	then
s	well
s	well done
s	wow
s	yes

THE WORLD AROUND US

f	air
s	beach
f	bridge
f	castle
f	cave
m	city
m	country(side)
f	desert
f	environment
m	field
f	fire
m	forest
f	future
m	grass
m	ground
f	hill
m	island
m	jungle
m	lake
m	leaf/leaves
m	moon
m	mountain
f	planet
m	plant
f	pyramid
m	river
m	road
m	rock
s	sand
s	sea
s	shell
f	sky
f	space
m	star
s	street
s	sun
m	town
s	tree
m	village
s	water
m	waterfall
f	wood
m	world

ADJECTIVES

m	afraid
m	all
m	all right
s	angry
m	awake
m	back
m	bad
s	beautiful
m	best
m	better
s	big
f	bored
m	boring
m	bottom
f	brave
f	broken
m	busy
m	careful
f	cheap
s	clean
m	clever
s	closed
m	cloudy
m	cold
s	correct
f	dangerous
f	dark
f	dear
m	different

m	difficult
s	dirty
s	double
f	dry
f	each
f	early
m	easy
f	empty
s	English
f	enough
m	every
f	excellent
f	excited
m	exciting
f	expensive
f	extinct
m	famous
f	far
f	fast
m	fat
s	favourite
m	fine
m	first
f	friendly
f	front
f	full
f	fun
s	funny
f	glass
f	gold
s	good
s	great
f	half
s	happy
f	hard
f	heavy
s	her
f	high
s	his
f	horrible
m	hot
m	hungry
f	ill
f	important
f	interesting
s	its
f	kind
m	last
f	late
f	left (as in direction)
f	light
f	little
s	long
m	loud
f	lovely
f	low
f	many
f	married

f	metal
f	missing
m	more
m	most
s	my
m	naughty
s	new
f	next
s	nice
f	noisy
s	old
s	open
f	other
s	our
f	paper
f	plastic
f	poor
m	quick
m	quiet
f	ready
f	rich
s	right (correct)
f	right (as in direction)
m	round
s	sad
f	same
m	second
s	short
f	silver
f	single
m	slow
s	small
f	soft
s	sorry
f	spotted
m	square
m	straight
f	strange
f	striped
m	strong
f	sure
m	surprised
m	tall
m	terrible
s	their
m	thin
m	third
m	thirsty
f	tidy
m	tired
m	top
s	ugly
f	unfriendly
f	unhappy
f	untidy
f	warm
m	weak
m	well

m wet
m windy
m worse
m worst
m wrong
s young
s your

DETERMINERS

s a/an
f a few
f a little
s a lot of
m all
m another
m any
m both
f each
m every
s lots of
s many
m more
m most
f much
s my
s no
s one
f other
s some
s that
s the
s these
s this
s those

ADVERBS

s a lot
f after
s again
f ago
m all right
f already
f also
m always
f anywhere
f away
m back
m badly
f before
m best
m better
m carefully
m down
m downstairs
f early
f else
f ever

f everywhere
f far
f fast
m first
f hard
s here
m how
m how much
m how often
m inside
f just
m last
f late
f later
s lots
m loudly
m more
m most
f much
m near
m never
f next
s not
s now
f nowhere
f of course (not)
m off
m often
m on
f once
m only
m out
m outside
f over
f perhaps
m quickly
m quietly
m slowly
f so
m sometimes
f somewhere
f soon
f still
f straight on
f suddenly
s then
s there
s today
f together
f tomorrow
f tonight
s too
f twice
m up
m upstairs
f usually
s very
m well

m when
m worse
m worst
m yesterday
f yet

PREPOSITIONS

s about
m above
f across
m after
s at
m before
s behind
m below
s between
m by
m down
f during
f far
s for
f for (prep of time)
f from
m in (prep of time)
s in front of
m inside
f into
s like
m near
s next to
s of
m off
s on
m on (prep of time)
m opposite
m out of
m outside
f over
f past
m round
f since
m than
f through
s to
s under
f until
s with
f without

CONJUNCTIONS

f after
s and
m because
f before
s but
f if
s or

f so
m than
m when

PRONOUNS

m all
m another
f anyone
f anything
m both
f each
f else
f enough
f everyone
f everything
s he
s her
s hers
s him
s his
s I
s it
s its
s me
s mine
m more
m most
f much
f no-one
m nothing
s one
f other
s ours
s she
f someone
m something
s that
s theirs
s them
s these
s they
s this
s those
s us
s we
f where
m which
m who
s you
s yours

VERBS

Irregular:
s be
f begin
f break
m bring

f burn
m buy
s catch (a ball)
m catch (a bus)
s choose
s come
f cut
s do
s draw
s drink
s drive
s eat
f fall
f fall over
f feel (like)
s find
f find out
s fly
f forget
s get
f get (off/on/to)
m get (un)dressed
m get up
s give
s go
f go out
m go shopping
f grow
s have
s have (got)
m have (got) to
f hear
m hide
s hit
s hold
m hurt
s know
s learn
f leave
s let
f let's
f lie (down)
m lose
s make
m mean
f meet
m must
s put
m put on
s read
s ride
s run
s say
s see
f sell
f send
s sing
s sit (down)

s sleep
f smell (v intr)
f smell (like) (v tr)
f speak
s spell
f spend
s stand (up)
f steal
s swim
f swing
m take
m take (a bus)
m take (a photo)
m take off
f take time
f teach
s tell
m think
s throw
s understand
m wake up
s wear
f will
f win
f won't
s write

Regular:
s add
f agree
s answer
f arrive
s ask
f ask for
f believe
s bounce
f brush
f burn
m call
f camp
m carry
s clean
m climb
s close
s colour
f comb
s complete
m cook
s cross
m cry
m dance
f decide
m dream
m drop
m email
f end
s enjoy
f explain

f fetch
m film
f finish
m fish
f follow
f glue
f guess
f happen
f hate
m help
m hop
m invite
s jump
s kick
m laugh
s learn
s like
s listen (to)
s live
s look
f look after
s look at
m look for
f look (like)
s love
f mind
f mix
m move
m need
s open
s paint
s phone
s pick up
m plant
s play (with)
s point
s point to
f post
f prefer
f pull
f push
f race
m rain
f remember
m sail
f score
m shop
m shout
s show
m skate
f ski
m skip
f sledge
s smile
m snow
f sound (like)
s start
f stay

s stop
f study
s talk
f taste (like)
s test
m text
f thank
s tick
f tidy
s try
f turn
f turn (off/on)
f use
m video
f visit
m wait
s walk
s want
m wash
s watch
s wave
f whisper
f whistle
f wish
m work

MODALS

s can/cannot/can't
m could
f may
f might
m must
m shall
f should
m would

QUESTION WORDS

s how
s how many
m how much
s how old
s what
m when
s where
s which
s who
s whose
m why

NAMES

s Alex
s Ann
s Anna
s Ben
f Betty
s Bill

m Daisy
f David
f Emma
m Fred
f Harry
f Helen
m Jack
m Jane
s Jill
m Jim
m John
f Katy
s Kim
s Lucy
m Mary
s May
f Michael
s Nick
s Pat
m Paul
m Peter
f Richard
f Robert
m Sally
s Sam
f Sarah
s Sue
s Tom
s Tony
m Vicky
f William